I0820480

READ MY MIND

First published in 2025 by OH
An Imprint of HEADLINE PUBLISHING GROUP LIMITED

1

Disclaimer:
This book has not been licensed, approved, sponsored, or endorsed by Sabrina Carpenter.

Cataloguing in Publication Data is available from the British Library

ISBN 978-1-03542-721-5

Compiled and written by: Malcolm Croft
Editorial: Saneaah Muhammad
Designed and typeset in Avenir by: Stephen Cary
Project manager: Russell Porter
Production: Arlene Lestrade
Printed and bound in Dubai

Headline's policy is to use papers that are natural, renewable and recyclable products and made from wood grown in well-managed forests and other controlled sources. The logging and manufacturing processes are expected to conform to the environmental regulations of the country of origin.

HEADLINE PUBLISHING GROUP LIMITED
An Hachette UK Company
Carmelite House, 50 Victoria Embankment, London EC4Y 0DZ

The authorised representative in the EEA is Hachette Ireland, 8 Castlecourt Centre, Dublin 15, D15 XTP3, Ireland (email: info@hbgi.ie)

www.headline.co.uk www.hachette.co.uk

READ MY MIND

THE LITTLE GUIDE TO SABRINA CARPENTER

UNOFFICIAL AND UNAUTHORIZED

CONTENTS

INTRODUCTION

For ten years now, Sabrina Carpenter has entertained her fans, transforming in front of their eyes from a short and sweet tween Disney princess into America's No. 1 Best New Female Artist – if her six Grammy Award nominations and first ever Grammy wins at the 2025 ceremony are anything to go by. From the mere age of 14 when she received her first shot at small-screen success and first recording contract at the same time, Sabrina has been capable of shapeshifting her sound and style from country ballad to hip-hop-flavoured synth-pop-bop and dramatic tear-jerker to comedic genius in less time than it takes to walk her slight height. Today, her petite feet are firmly set in both the acting and singing worlds, with opportunities to feed both in no short supply… and what she does next is anyone's guess.

What we do know, however, is that over the summer of 2024, Sabrina's string of hit singles from her sixth album, *Short n' Sweet*, dominated global airwaves so loudly that even her friend and mentor Taylor Swift called it the "Summer of Sabrina". A plethora of other peers have sung the singer's praise too, from Beyoncé to Adele, Shania to Christina and Selena to Billie – admiring her classy leap from child star to award-winning songwriter without losing her sense of self.

Read My Mind is every "Sabrinators" dream. It's a tiny tome filled with all the wisdom, wit and iconic quips that you would expect from a superstar with more than *10 billion* global total streams – 5 billion in 2024 alone! With so much already accomplished, and with so much more she wants to achieve, Sabrina Carpenter looks set to become the most influential and innovative icon of her generation and a voice we'll all be yearning to listen to for several decades to come.

Enjoy!

CHAPTER ONE

WORLD MEETS GIRL

Sabrina's sensational overnight success in 2024 was a result of a decade-long commitment to manifesting her destiny.

It all began in 2014 when, aged 14, she signed her first recording contract and was cast to star in 72 episodes of Disney's highly acclaimed *Girl Meets World*. Since then, Sabrina's feet haven't touched the ground.

Next stop: World domination…

For the people who love those early records and listen to them, I love you for that. But I personally feel a sense of separation from them, largely due to the shift in who I am as a person and as an artist, pre-pandemic and post-pandemic.

Sabrina, on her earlier records on the Disney Hollywood label before signing with Island Records in 2021, *Variety*, August 6, 2024

"I knew that I wouldn't be able to thrive as a recording artist the same way I would have been able to working on a show as a child actor, which I know sounds weird to have that perspective at 12, but I was really lucky to."

Sabrina, on signing her first record deal with Disney's Hollywood Records before she agreed to star in her debut Disney TV show *Girl Meets World*, *Time* magazine, October 2, 2024

August 4, 2009

The day Sabrina posted her first ever video on YouTube – she was just 10 years old!

The video was a cover of Taylor Swift's "Picture to Burn". It features Sabrina belting it out straight to camera, no frills, no effects, just pure singing talent in her homemade singing studio. It now has more than 1.7 million views.

Sabrina's next upload – two years later, in September 2011 – was a cover of Adele's "Set Fire to the Rain". It now has more than 9 million views.

“

I’ve been working since I was a kid. I didn’t have time to go to prom, or have a crazy summer vacation in France. So I allow myself to live life to the fullest, to feel everything in the moment, and embrace the fact that, right now, I’m only 25.

”

Sabrina, on living her life her way regardless of her being a celebrity, Apple Music 1, August 23, 2024

When I was around 11, I booked my first role, and it was a much more serious role than I ever thought I'd be doing, but I think that's what showed me that there was maybe a career in it.

”

Sabrina, on her first acting role*, *Cliché* magazine, December 9, 2015

* The role was intense: Sabrina portrayed a victim of sexual abuse for an episode of *Law and Order: Special Victims Unit*.

I was too young. When your voice hasn't gone through puberty, maybe you shouldn't be making music.

Sabrina, on her debut single, the ukulele-driven "Can't Blame a Girl For Trying", created when she was just 14, *Dork* magazine, March 22, 2023

I was six years old. I can remember watching the pilot episode of *Hannah Montana*. I was like, 'You can do that?! For a career? Sing, dance, act?' That was the moment I realized I really wanted to do it. I didn't know if I would get to, but that was the moment where I was like, wait... That's a job. I'm still working on it.

Sabrina, on when she knew she wanted to entertain people for a living, *The Face*, February 25, 2022

I troll myself daily when people tag me in clips from *Girl Meets World*. I was so proud to be a part of it and everything that it stood for but I definitely would have done some things different had I been doing it now. I think the beauty of the show was that we really were at the age that we were playing and we were coming into ourselves as we were playing characters that were coming into themselves.

”

Sabrina, on her role of Maya in *Girl Meets World* and making different creative choices as an actor with hindsight, *Teen Vogue*, August 17, 2020

Hometown Glory

Sabrina is the only famous person to come from her hometown of East Greenville, in the Keystone State, Pennsylvania. (The state itself has produced a plethora of top talent, from Will Smith to Joan Jett to P!nk, as well as Sabrina's idols Christina Aguilera and Taylor Swift).

Sabrina was born and raised in the small rural town – with a population of just 2,000 – with her parents, Elizabeth and David, and three older sisters, Shannon, Sarah and Cayla.

I look at *Emails I Can't Send* as a first album for me in many ways. Many of my best friends would listen to songs on this album and say, 'This sounds like the way you speak to me. This sounds like your sense of humour, whereas maybe other projects sounded like you were trying to be someone else.' And that's fine. I didn't know who I was at 12. That's okay.

Sabrina, on her earliest albums compared to 2022's *Emails I Can't Send*, *Glamour*, March 17, 2023

That was my childhood in every way, shape and form. I grew up on that set, I grew up around those people and luckily they were very kind-hearted, intelligent people that definitely gave me the ability to experiment. And I definitely credit a lot of what I do now and where I am because of that show and that character I got to play. So, yeah, a very, very special project.

Sabrina, on playing the role of Maya Hart on *Girl Meets World*, *J-14*, June 23, 2020

When people become familiar with you as a child, it's really hard for them to see you be a woman all of a sudden. But I have never tried to rush or force the process of growing up. I feel like I've grown up when I've felt like I should and not when other people felt like I should.

Sabrina, on growing up in the spotlight, March 17, 2023

I met Miley Cyrus when I was 10 years old. *Hannah Montana* was a huge influence in my life so I was pretty starstruck. I wish I could tell you some advice she gave me but I literally had never been so speechless in my life.

”

Sabrina, on meeting her idol Miley Cyrus, *KODE* magazine, December 2015

I think it's very easy for people to look at kids that come from Disney and see them as a face and not really a voice. I want my fans to be able to learn something from something that I did.

Sabrina, on being a role model to her fans and not just a "glossy pop star", *Refinery29*, August 5, 2019

May 11, 1999

Sabrina's birthday is actually quite an important day in history. It is the day that Constantine the Great, in 330, named the rebuilt city of Byzantium Rome – it was built in a day! – and declared it the capital of the Roman Empire.

It is also the birthday of Salvador Dalí, the famed Spanish surrealist painter.

I hate to sound cliché, but I'm just being myself. I feel like a lot of my personality has been infused in my music that wouldn't have made sense to people two or three years ago. The jokes land a bit better.

Sabrina, on mixing her new music with her sense of humour, *Vogue*, August 30, 2024

"I love Christina Aguilera. She was my very first idol and icon. I was 11 years old and you couldn't get her name out of my mouth. She's very special to me. Her songs raised me."

Sabrina, on the singer that inspired her the most, *Paper* magazine, August 21, 2024

That's the cool thing about being a kid in the industry. You have so much vulnerability and curiosity because you don't know what you're doing until you're a couple years in. But I still don't know what I'm doing. I'm just pretending that I do.

Sabrina, on faking it until you make it, *Cliché* magazine, December 9, 2015

I was that kid who never had a back-up plan. I just knew the one thing that I always wanted to do.

”

Sabrina, on manifesting her destiny to be a songwriter and performer, *Student Pocket Guide*, June 19, 2018

My advice to my younger self is: Don't take other people's opinions more seriously than your own. I'd also probably say wear less eye make-up, but today I'm wearing loads so I've already failed.

Sabrina, when asked "What advice would you give to your 16-year old self?", *GQ*, February 25, 2022

I had a really dangerous Zac Efron phase. When I was 12 years old, and I was on a beach for the Fourth of July, I saw him and said, 'I'm a big fan of your work!' He gave me a hug. And I remember thinking, *Oh my god – he wasn't wearing a shirt and he gave me a hug!* I was like, 'This is amazing. I'm never washing my body!'

Sabrina, on her love for Zac Efron, *W magazine*, September 5, 2024

They never told me to stop singing. And that, psychologically, helped me become who I am.

Sabrina, on her parents, Elizabeth and David Carpenter, and their support, *CBS News*, October 6, 2024

I'm 900 inappropriate jokes away from being a Disney actor, but people still see me that way. I'm always extremely flattered to be grouped in with the other women and girls who I've idolized and looked up to who came from that world, but I feel very distant from it.

”

Sabrina, on forever being seen as a Disney Child Actor, *Variety*, August 6, 2024

The mistakes lead you to knowing yourself the most. If I didn't wear the hideous things I wore when I was 13, whatever fedora I had, I don't think I would've been the same person I am today. Also, what a humbling experience to look back and be like, 'I've changed'. That's a really good sign that you've lived life the way you should.

”

Sabrina, on learning from her mistakes, *Interview* magazine, February 8, 2024

I did my first audition when I was 11 years old. The first job that I booked – *Law & Order: SVU* – I was thrown off by that booking because I always wanted to do comedy. And on that show, I was a victim. I remember running the lines with my dad and asking, 'Is this what acting is?' And then I booked *Orange Is the New Black*. That episode was called 'Fucksgiving'. I went from raunchy to Disney!

”

Sabrina, on the genre range of her earliest acting auditions, *W* magazine, September 5, 2024

"

I rehearsed for about three months in New York, and we opened our first two nights, and then COVID humbled me – humbled me very quickly! I had been training to do eight shows a week. And now it's just – silence.

"

Sabrina, on her ill-fated starring role in Tina Fey's Broadway hit, *Mean Girls*, which was closed due to COVID-19 lockdown protocols, *CBS News*, October 6, 2024

When I was younger a lot of people assumed it was my parents' dream that they were trying to fulfil through me, and I always had to tell people it really had nothing to do with anyone but my 11-year-old self. I started writing my debut album as a child.

Sabrina, on having musical ambition from an early age, *Interview* magazine, February 8, 2024

My music is definitely in the world of pop. I'm a young girl, so I'm writing my songs and kind of growing up in this new generation where we change every five minutes. I'm definitely coming into who I am as an artist right now.

Sabrina, on her generation, and the transience of pop music, *Student Pocket Guide*, June 19, 2018

All of my music is autobiographical. I think when I was younger, it was a little harder for me to, like, pull everything from my own experiences, because my experiences were, like, doing school, going to the grocery store, being on set. It wasn't very exciting and it didn't give me a lot of inspiration to pull from. What I really wanted to do in the last few years was fully live and experience some actual real-life shit, and it happened, that's for sure.

Sabrina, on living a life less ordinary for the sake of her songwriting, *GQ*, February 25, 2022

I wasn't grinding and working for hours on end as a child, but I always felt I had a point to prove.

Sabrina, on signing with Disney's Hollywood Records at the same time she landed the role of Maya in the Disney-produced *Girl Meets World* – aged 12, *Variety*, August 6, 2024

There's something so interesting about how the world has changed, and now I see so much pressure being put on people's first and second projects. And to look at it in my kind of situation, I got really lucky. It's not that the other albums were throwaways for me, but they were definitely me, really not knowing who I was yet. So it's not that I don't feel connected to those albums, but they were made when I wasn't connected to myself.

”

Sabrina, on her earliest Disney-released albums, *Glamour*, March 17, 2023

"I'll put it this way: when I was younger, I was told by a lot of grown men that I needed to pick a genre, stay in that genre, be that genre and do one thing. I was 12. I know that sounds insane, but that was put into my head. So I think secretly my entire life, the goal was to be able to create something that felt multi-genre but also so distinctly myself."

Sabrina, on the opinions of the male-orientated music industry – and ignoring them, *Paper* magazine, August 21, 2024

Boy Meets World was my go-to, 8:00 A.M. before school. It was my go-to in the morning… It was a show that I always remembered just loving.

”

Sabrina, on being a fan of Disney's *Boy Meets World*, the predecessor of her breakout show *Girl Meets World*, *J-14*, June 23, 2020

“

I wrote most of the songs on *Emails I Can't Send* not intending to ever put them out in the world, because I don't think I would've written those songs if I thought about other people hearing them.

”

Sabrina, on the lyrical content of the songs on her 2022 album *Emails I Can't Send*, *Interview* magazine, February 8, 2024

The most common name for Sabrina fans is "Carpenters".

However, some fans also call themselves "Sabrinators".

Which one are you?

“

I had to go through puberty in such a public way. People have proof. Fans have pictures of me on Monday, Tuesday, Wednesday, Thursday, Friday. I don't love that, and while I'm very grateful of what I do, I would love to change that.

”

Sabrina, on social media, fans and fame, *GQ*, February 25, 2022

I was in a ghost town that had one little creperie down the road. I had my shot of espresso, and then I might have had some champagne, and before I knew it the song was written. I definitely hear it now in every car I get into, and being on the radio, to me, is still – it's like fate.

Sabrina, on writing "Espresso", *W* magazine, September 5, 2024

I wrote my first song when I was 10 years old and it was very bad. But over time, writing became a necessity for me; if I didn't write a song, I wouldn't be able to make it through these situations in life. I'm very lucky that I now get to do it all the time.

Sabrina, on her desire to be a songwriter above all else, grammys.com, December 20, 2023

CHAPTER TWO

DOUBLE TROUBLE

Singer. Songwriter. Musician. Actress. Producer. Influencer. Fashion model. Empire builder. Comedic genius.

What Sabrina lacks in size she makes up for in adding many sparkly strings to her bow. As a versatile, dynamic actor and a show-stopping soprano, Sabrina is capable of entertaining audiences on screens and stages, both great and small. She may not look it, but she's double the trouble...

I go to the movies and I get really jealous of the people in the movies. I'm like, 'Oh, I want to be in a movie.' And then I go to concerts and I get jealous of people onstage. I'm like, 'Oh, I want to be onstage.' I think that's a good sign.

Sabrina, on her ambitions to conquer song, stage and screen, *Cosmopolitan*, May 17, 2024

My character is Maya Hart. She is the troublemaker of life. The cool thing about her is she has got this guard around her. She has got this force field around her and I think that is why she has this tough sarcastic humour. She kind of uses that to hide over her family life. It's cool and she is a really dimensional character, and she is really fun to play.

”

Sabrina, on Maya Hart, her character in *Girl Meets World*, alexandriamclean.com, July 14, 2015

Nobody really knows what they're doing and nobody has it all figured out. Some people might act like they do, but even they don't. Even the strongest, most amazing, confident and powerful people have their moments. Knowing that has really enhanced my life, for sure. It made things a little easier when I was being really hard on myself.

”

Sabrina, when asked "What's a piece of advice that changed your life?", *The Face*, February 25, 2022

People wrote me off from my past as a Disney kid, but when you reach a certain place you've always wanted to be at there's a whole new group of people that want to try to bring you down.

Sabrina, on having haters no matter what she does,
The Guardian, August 23, 2024

Since her debut TV performance in 2011, Sabrina has appeared in several TV shows either as a main star or cameo and in 10 films as a starring role. Check them out!

1. *Noobz* (2012)
2. *Horns* (2013)
3. *The Hate U Give* (2018)
4. *The Short History of the Long Road* (2019)
5. *Tall Girl* (2019)
6. *Work It* (2020)
7. *Clouds* (2020)
8. *Tall Girl 2* (2022)
9. *Emergency* (2022)
10. *A Nonsense Christmas with Sabrina Carpenter* (2024)

“

For a long time, I was constantly guided and misguided. I’m so grateful for all of those times where I was led astray, because now I’m a lot more equipped going into situations where I have to trust my own instincts.

”

Sabrina, on learning from her mistakes early in her career, *Time* magazine, October 2, 2024

If you want to call me a Polly Pocket, a Bratz doll, I don't care. You'll meet me and then you'll be like, damn, she talks a lot more than the dolls do.

”

Sabrina, on her petite stature, *Time* magazine, October 2, 2024

I thrive on doing many different things and feeling creatively like I am using every outlet at my disposal. Luckily for me, I've had the opportunity to do that with my music and different projects within the acting world but I don't feel like I've accomplished half of the things that I want to in both of those areas.

Sabrina, on her future musical and acting ambitions, *Student Pocket Guide*, June 19, 2018

I had to fight off a lot of voices and opinions and people controlling me when I was younger, whether that be in music or acting, because I was a child coming into this.

Sabrina, on her formative years in the entertainment industry, *Paper* magazine, August 21, 2024

I put it this way: music is my own voice, music is my stories and I have complete control. And with acting, I get to tell other people's stories, and I get to put myself in someone else's shoes, and I really, really get to feel what they're feeling, and hopefully contribute something else to this world in a way that I can't do with my music. So I love both.

Sabrina, on her love of acting and music, katewaterhouse.com, September 9, 2018

I was lucky to come into a show that was dealing with real-life issues, and obviously putting a lighter spin on things because you do want that optimism – although our writers never spoke down to the audience. My character had very real circumstances – a father who left the family when my character was five years old, and now has another family, and a mother that was a bit unstable and didn't have a job. They were really trying to address real-life issues and things actually happening in so many kids' lives.

”

Sabrina, on joining *Girl Meets World*, and the realness of her character Maya Hart, *Hero* magazine, July 2, 2018

I've always felt really comfortable in my own skin. Even when I was 12 years old auditioning. I was fearless. I had no apprehension going into rooms with total strangers. I felt very comfortable with rejection.

Sabrina, on being fearless when she was younger, *Elle*, August 11, 2020

I'm not gonna say I peed my pants because that sounds really graphic and maybe not sanitary, but… it was very much a childhood dream come true. I still probably have not processed it if I'm being completely honest with you.

99

Sabrina, when Taylor Swift revealed that Sabrina would be the opening act for the South America and Australia dates of her world-record-breaking Eras tour*, whowhatwear.com, November 15, 2023.

* For her tour debut in Mexico City, Sabrina opened her performance with her first ever YouTube upload, a video of her nine-year-old self singing Swift's "Picture to Burn".

"I just love creating music – there's sort of a need for it – and when that's the thing that's driving you, success doesn't really matter. You're just gonna keep going regardless. I've been called a flop many times but I'm still here."

Sabrina, on her desire to create music regardless of fame and popularity, *The Guardian*, August 23, 2024

I was completely alone in wanting to release 'Espresso' as a single. There was a lot of questioning from the powers above behind whether it made sense. But they trusted me in the end, and I was happy that I believed in myself at that moment.

Sabrina, on releasing "Espresso" as a single, *Variety*, August 6, 2024

"Espresso" was the most-streamed song in the world in 2024, with more than 1.7 billion streams, and has amassed more than 300 million views on YouTube in just three months.

It also went to No. 1 in more than 30 countries and received the MTV Video Music Award for Song of the Year – Sabrina's first VMA win. She also earned a Grammy Award nomination for Record of the Year and won Best Pop Solo Performance, both for "Espresso", at the 67th Annual Grammy Awards in 2025.

If your favourite song is 'Espresso', then you'll have another song that you love. And if your favourite song is 'Please Please Please', you'll have another song that you love. And if you hate both of those songs, then listen to a different album.

Sabrina, on the songs on her 2024 album *Short n' Sweet*, *Paper* magazine, August 21, 2024

I literally get to sing into a microphone. That's my job. It's everything that I've always wanted.

Sabrina, on her dream job, whowhatwear.com, November 15, 2023

The more I'm honest with myself, the more other people feel like it forces them to be honest with me as well.

”

Sabrina, on the importance of honesty and being true to herself, *Glamour*, March 17, 2023

I didn't feel any singular pressure on myself because I was coming into a new show as a new character that nobody knew. That gave me the creativity to build Maya's personality and quirks. Coming into the cast of a show that made such a permanent mark on the world and held seven seasons under their belt was intimidating, but they welcomed us like family.

Sabrina, on being cast as Maya Hart for Disney's *Girl Meets World*, *Kode* magazine, December 2015

> "I think a misperception is that I don't write my music. I think a lot of people think because I have, you know, a producer and co-writers that I love, that I'm sitting in the room on my phone, not writing songs."

Sabrina, on misconceptions about her, *CBS News*, October 6, 2024

When people ask me now 'Why do you want to do this?' they expect there to be some really introspective, larger than life response and, truthfully, I do it because it's fun.

Sabrina, on the reason why she's a performer, *GQ*, February 25, 2022

The Next Miley Cyrus Project

In 2009, aged 10, Sabrina entered the nationwide singing competition *The Next Miley Cyrus Project*, judged by Cyrus herself.

The competition searched throughout the United States for the next bright star. Although Carpenter came third, she turned so many heads in her auditions that she was given a contract with Disney that launched her career as a singer and an actor.

I remember watching *The Next Miley Cyrus Project* and being like 'I want to do that. I want to sing, and I want to act, and I want to dance. I want to do all those things.'

Sabrina, on entering the competition, *People*, June 2024

Acting and singing was all I wanted. It was all my doing, and sure people might be like, 'How did you know at that age?' But I knew.

Sabrina, on her confidence of knowing what she wanted to do as a career – from age six, *GQ*, February 25, 2022

If I'm having a bad day, or didn't get enough sleep, or haven't had any coffee, and I say something and the tone comes off a little snarky, there's a million people waiting to call you a terrible person. You've got to tiptoe around the edge of being authentic and protecting yourself, which is a bit of a mindfuck.

Sabrina, on the perils and pitfalls of online trolls and internet-age fame, *The Guardian*, August 23, 2024

I have all these movies in my head when I write songs. Growing up making movies and TV shows has made me really fascinated with cinematography, wardrobes, characters and theatrics. When it comes to telling a narrative of my own experiences in my life, I want it to be really cinematic.

”

Sabrina, on the cinematic nature of her songs and her songwriting, *GQ*, February 25, 2022

Short and Sweet

At 5ft, Sabrina Carpenter may be petite in size, but her voice sure packs a powerful punch. Nor is she alone in the Short and Sweet Singers Club.

1. 5ft 5in – Selena Gomez
2. 5ft 4in – Britney Spears
3. 5ft 3in – Billie Eilish
4. 5ft 3in – Charli XCX
5. 5ft 2in – Lady Gaga
6. 5ft 2in – Cardi B
7. 5ft 2in – Camila Cabello
8. 5ft 1in – Christina Aguilera
9. 5ft ½in – Ariana Grande
10. 5ft – Sabrina Carpenter

"I'm so blunt and forward. It'll probably bite me in the ass at some point but it's been a really therapeutic album to be able to just say what I'm thinking. Sometimes men embarrass you. That's super normal."

Sabrina, on the lyrical meaning of her hit song "Please Please Please", *Time* magazine, October 2, 2024

I have dreams and goals, and I will say I'm a little bit of a freak manifester sometimes, which is a blessing and a curse depending on how you look at it. I always knew deep down that this was something I would do with my life, and I didn't ever really doubt that, even when shit was hitting the ceiling fan.

Sabrina, on making her musical dreams come true with the power of her own belief, *Paper* magazine, August 21, 2024

There's beautiful sides to fame and there's really dark, weird sides to it.

Sabrina, on the scrutiny and hate that is part and parcel of the music industry and fame, *The Guardian*, August 23, 2024

“

I think it’s important to play characters like Hailey just as much as it is to play the down-to-earth, fun-loving, go-lucky kind of girls. Because people will see themselves in each one, and then hopefully take something from it.

”

Sabrina, on her performance as Hailey in *The Hate U Give* (2018), *Teen Vogue*, August 17, 2020

I remember vividly as a child watching *The Wizard of Oz* and seeing Judy Garland. I remember hearing that this was the first film in colour and, because it was the first, the colours were so bright and vivid. It sounds really weird, but watching that film, I was entranced. I didn't know what acting was, I didn't know *how* to act, but I was definitely very interested in what was in front of me and I wanted to be involved.

”

Sabrina, on when she knew she wanted to be an actor, *Hero* magazine, July 2, 2018

“

Little baby Sabs! They put no make-up on me – I was like a tomato!

”

Sabrina, looking back at her first ever TV role on *Law and Order: Special Victims Unit*, live-manchester.co.uk, June 4, 2017

I was always performing as a child, anytime there was a stage or an elevated hill that I could pretend was a stage, I was straight to it. I think there's just an energy that you can't really get anywhere else after, doing a show.

”

Sabrina, on her love of performance art, *GQ*, February 25, 2022

I feel really grateful that this has happened over the course of a lot of time of me figuring it out because it doesn't feel like it was sprung up on me. It's almost like I can just relax and be excited about it. Sabrina wasn't built in a day.

Sabrina, on her slow and steady ten-year rise to global superstardom, *Rolling Stone*, June 17, 2024

My fans have always been there for me, right by my side since day one. It's one of the best feelings in the world to look into the crowd and see those faces you've seen before, and it feels like I've got friends out there in the audience I'm performing for.

Sabrina, on her love of her loyal and dedicated fans, interview with bakchormeeboy.com, April 12, 2019

"That, to me, has been special to watch – for people to embrace the universe I've been building for the last couple of years. For them to enjoy the music and my sense of humour has been really beautiful, and I'm so grateful."

Sabrina, on her fans falling in love with her after her release from Disney, *Vogue*, August 30, 2024

Even though I've got older sisters, and I'm the baby of the family, I think I came out of the womb with an older mentality. I've always had this kind of 'take charge' mentality and it was never my parents 'forcing' me into doing things, but me pushing my parents and telling them that this is what I've wanted.

”

Sabrina, on knowing precisely what she wants, bakchormeeboy.com, April 12, 2019

I write songs about exactly how I feel, so I guess I can't be so surprised that people are interested in who and what those songs are about. That's something that comes with the territory.

Sabrina, on her fans spreading rumours as to the meaning, or persons, implied in her lyrics, *Rolling Stone*, June 17, 2024

I always believe that my songs write themselves and find their place in this world because they need to be there, rather than the other way around. Every feeling that has inspired me to write has been something strong enough that I felt compelled to say something about it.

Sabrina, on her emotion-led songwriting process,
The Face, February 25, 2022

“

My career has come together very organically and I’ve enjoyed where my life has taken me to so far. I think if I released an album at age 12, I’d probably have regretted it immensely. Even listening to *Eyes Wide Open* now, the album I released at 16, I already feel like it doesn’t feel like the me I am today. But I do recognize that it was a version of myself I was at one point, and honestly, I regret nothing.

”

Sabrina, on her career choices and her earliest musical offerings, bakchormeeboy.com, April 12, 2019

CHAPTER THREE

ESPRESSO TO GO-GO

Armed with more than sixty synth-pop bops in her musical arsenal, Sabrina is well-equipped to take over the world's airwaves.

However, with the release of *Short n' Sweet*, the singer was sent into the stratosphere with a collection of summer-soaked tunes – from "Taste" to "Nonsense", "Please Please Please" to "Bed Chem" and "Juno" to "Espresso" – that now define her as the queen of pop.

2024 was the summer of Sabrina, and it was a hot one indeed…

Sometimes I get insecure about pop music and the fact that it can't always resonate with people. So it was really special for me to experience 'Nonsense' having its own life, maybe because it felt like the closest to my true personality, as silly as that sounds.

”

Sabrina, on the viral nature of her first big hit "Nonsense" and its raunchy ad-libbed lyrics when performed live, *Interview* magazine, February 4, 2024

'Nonsense' happened like a storm in my life, so I didn't really have time to consider one too many dick jokes. I've written literally 900 outros. I've said a lot of provocative things that I don't do or feel – and now I need rhymes, I'm running low!

Sabrina, on the viral sensation of her often controversial "Nonsense" outros, *The Guardian*, August 23, 2024

The 'Nonsense' outros were a happy accident. I didn't sit around a table of marketing people who said, 'You know what you should do every night?' It was literally my sister and I that were like 'I have all these extra lines from the song. Let's shout out the city!' Then it took on a life of its own.

Sabrina, on the viral phenomenon that became the somewhat scandalous "Nonsense" outros, *Paper* magazine, August 21, 2024

> There's just so much good music coming out, so the fact that I put 'Espresso' out in April and people are still considering it the song of the summer... You don't get an award for something like this, it's something you just know in your soul. So it's very, very sweet, and I'm so happy that everybody has given it life and longevity through clever memes and all the things I've seen.

Sabrina, on the global success and viral quality of "Espresso", *Vogue*, August 30, 2024

Singular is the beginning of me finding my voice. Act II is going to be different from Act I, only in the sense that each song is different in its own right. The through line remains the same, and I still maintain the same voice and confidence on both albums.

Sabrina, on her third and fourth albums *Singular Act I* and *Act II*, her final albums for Disney before signing to Island Records, bakchormeeboy.com, April 12, 2019

I believe in divine timing, I always have. There are moments in everyone's life where the stars align. But it wouldn't have happened if I hadn't spent the last years working so hard.

Sabrina, on her belief that her time to shine is now for a reason, *Paper* magazine, August 21, 2024

Essential Playlist #1: Most Popular

With more than 80 million monthly listeners, Sabrina is the current bop queen of Spotify streaming. These are her ten most popular tracks…

1. "Espresso" – 1.7 billon streams!
2. "Nonsense" – 1 billion streams!
3. "Please Please Please"
4. "On My Way"
5. "Feather"
6. "Taste"
7. "Looking at Me"
8. "Thumbs"
9. "because i liked a boy"
10. "Sue Me" – 250 million streams!

Being in the charts is not the reason I write music and it's not the reason I'll ever write music. It's like the sprinkles on top of the sundae.

Sabrina, on music charts and record-breaking sales numbers, *The Guardian*, August 23, 2024

I'm one of those people who sits in a room for hours just to make a second verse work and make it mean more than just filler fluff. To me, a song has to be this cohesive arc. Sometimes you get really lucky with songs, when you're listening to it, you can see this movie happening in my head. That's when I know it's a truly special song, and I've succeeded.

Sabrina, on working hard to create cohesive compositions, bakchormeeboy.com, April 12, 2019

Short n' Sweet wasn't supposed to just be a summer album; it's something that feels happy yet emotional, but there are times of the year when people really need songs that sound a certain way, and there's a few on this record that I think, going into autumn, randomly, are going to feel really, really nice.

Sabrina, on the "Summer of Sabrina" and the feelings that the songs on *Short n' Sweet* evoke, *Vogue*, August 30, 2024

The scariest thing in the world is getting up on a stage in front of that many people and having to perform as if it's nothing. If the one thing that helps you do that is the way you feel comfortable dressing, then that's what you've got to do.

Sabrina, on how she overcomes the fear of performing live, *Time* magazine, October 2, 2024

I'm trying to avoid calling this 'my dream album' because I don't think I would have been able to dream up this set of songs a couple years ago.

Sabrina, on her 2024 album *Short n' Sweet*, *Variety*, August 6, 2024

The amount of times I have been saved, inspired and rejuvenated by the art that other people have made is countless. As cheesy as it sounds, art saves the world one person at a time.

Sabrina, on the importance of art and creativity in the world as a force for good, *Time* magazine, October 2, 2024

My friend Paloma Sandoval and I coined the term 'Bed chem'. I went to the studio that day and was like, 'I have this title and idea, and we have to make it sexy and a little bit unserious at the same time because it is such a ridiculous concept.'

”

Sabrina, on "Bed Chem", *Paper* magazine, August 21, 2024

“I don’t love the idea that a pop star is someone who makes catchy songs with easy-to-grasp concepts. It resonates with part of me, but I grew up with Stevie Nicks and Dolly Parton and Carole King and Patsy Cline, and that music didn’t necessarily feel like pop to me.”

Sabrina, on the simplicity of pop music and pop stars producing music considered superficial, *Interview* magazine, February 8, 2024

I often think back to when Bruno Mars won six Grammies and said, 'I'm just getting started!' I hear that and I think, 'Wow, if that's just getting started, then I'm somewhere in the prequel of the prequel to getting started!' There are so many things I haven't done yet, so many places to go and so many people to meet. I just want to accomplish so much with my life, with so many songs yet to write and so many projects to embark on.

”

Sabrina, on her career just getting started!
Bakchormeeboy.com, April 12, 2019

“

Comparison is the thief of joy.

”

Sabrina, on being pitted against Olivia Rodrigo in the media after they deemed her a “home-wrecker” after she reportedly “stole” Rodrigo’s then-boyfriend Joshua Bassett, *Hunger* magazine, March 22, 2022

It was Olivia Rodrigo's beef with Sabrina in her 2021 hit song "drivers license" that propelled Sabrina into the limelight as "that blonde girl", and the girl who, according to Rodrigo, stole the heart of her then-boyfriend, Joshua Bassett*, whom she met on the set of *High School Musical: The Musical: The Series.*

Sabrina's response to Rodrigo's track, "because i liked a boy" contained several lyrics that revealed the death threats she received labelling her a "home-wrecker".

* Bassett came out as gay in 2021.

I like to keep my eyes and ears open for things that resonate with me because that's what brings my world to life. But most of the time I have absolutely no idea what I'm doing. The more I keep creating, the more ideas just come out of the woodwork.

”

Sabrina, on life events as an influence on musical inspiration, *Interview* magazine, February 8, 2024

"

I think the best thing about being famous is that you have an opportunity to speak to a really large audience and hopefully contribute to some of the growth in the world in a positive way, however you choose to.

"

Sabrina, on the positives of being famous and being a role model, katewaterhouse.com, September 9, 2018

To date, Sabrina has sold more than 10 million albums worldwide across six studio albums.

Which one is your favourite?

1. *Eyes Wide Open* (2015)
2. *Evolution* (2016)
3. *Singular: Act I* (2018)
4. *Singular: Act II* (2019)
5. *Emails I Can't Send* (2022)
6. *Short n' Sweet* (2024)

* In November 2024, Sabrina scored the Grammy nomination for Best New Artist at the Grammy Awards 2025 – one of six nominations in total – despite having already released six albums over the past 10 years!

I love visiting the kids while I'm on the road. It kind of takes me away from what I'm doing and makes me realize how lucky I am. And how lucky I am to have all these amazing people around me every day. The kids inspire me. I'm very excited to be working with them more hands on – they are such an incredible group of people.

Sabrina, on her ambassadorial role with the Ryan Seacrest Foundation, dedicated to inspiring youth through entertainment and education, live-manchester.co.uk, June 4, 2017

When you're 12 years old, it's so easy to be like, 'I want to be an actress and a singer, let's do it all!' because your metabolism is up, you don't need an espresso, your body is like, go, go, go!

”

Sabrina, on her young age allowing her to be both singer and actor at the same time, *Hero* magazine, July 2, 2018

I'm so, so lucky that it's happening at a time where I feel most aligned with myself. I feel more myself than I ever have, and that's something I'm really grateful for.

Sabrina, on the serendipitous timing of her rise to global fame, *Paper* magazine, August 21, 2024

I think you have to be twisted to like touring, so I think I'm really weird. It's very challenging, and I think that I've probably developed most of my anxiety from being on the road, but I think that when you come out of it, you're just a lot stronger.

”

Sabrina, on her love of touring and being on the road, katewaterhouse.com, September 9, 2018

In October 2024, Sabrina's hit song "Espresso" continued to go super viral on social media for many weeks, after it appeared in a *Saturday Night Live* (*SNL*) comedy sketch.

In the skit, Ariana Grande, as a bridesmaid, sang the song with changed lyrics, about the bride who she suspects is cheating on the groom, out of tune and off-key.

In an Instagram post on October 14, Carpenter said she loved the sketch and called it "very nice and on pitch".

I called the album *Short n' Sweet* for a number of reasons, not least because I'm short. I thought back on relationships, and felt like the short ones affected me the most. I looked back at my sometimes erratic behaviour. The moments and mistakes I allowed myself to make say a lot about my character.

Sabrina, on the inspiration behind the title of *Short n' Sweet*, Apple Music 1, August 23, 2024

Short n' Sweet is the hot older sister of *Emails I Can't Send*. It's my second 'big girl' album; it's a companion but it's not the same. When it comes to having full creative control and being a full-fledged adult, I would consider this a sophomore album.

Sabrina, on comparing her two "big girl" albums, *Short n' Sweet* and *Emails I Can't Send*, *Variety*, August 6, 2024

In September 2024, Sabrina's first three singles from *Short n' Sweet* – "Espresso", "Please Please Please" and "Taste" – all landed in the U.S. top five Billboard's Hot 100 chart in the same week.

Only one other musical act has achieved the same feat – the Beatles, in 1964.

When I was writing 'Espresso', I knew I loved it. I don't ever want to make myself sound like a psychic. All I knew was that I was faced with a decision of what song I wanted to put out into the world first when it came to this album, and I was like, 'I think this is the time for this song. This makes the most sense for me right now and where I'm at in life'.

Sabrina, on "Espresso" being the right song at the right time on Sabrina's quest for world domination, *Paper* magazine, August 21, 2024

CHAPTER FOUR

SWEET ATTITUDE

Sabrina's love for music and acting shines through in everything she does – writing heartfelt lyrics, creating songs that reflect her true self and performing with undeniable energy.

For her, it's all about connection, turning personal stories into music that resonates with fans around the world.

Sabrina's passion for her craft and gratitude for those who embrace her work make her journey as sweet and authentic as the songs she creates and the characters she inhibits.

Girl Meets World was a show based on historical moments, and with each episode we would tie in to a time in history when a similar situation happened between people. So, we got to cover bullying, religion, autism, feminism, broken families and broken homes. I can't tell you how many teenagers came up to me and told me, 'My mum left when I was seven years old, and you're the only character on television that I can relate to.'

”

Sabrina, on *Girl Meets World* episode storylines and her character resonating with viewers, *Hero* magazine, July 2, 2018

Emails I Can't Send, for me, is a time capsule of a special time in my life when I dealt with many things for the first time. I feel like I came out of that with a much greater perspective, and all these songs are based on real nights or experiences and reflecting and foreshadowing. There was a lot in between. So I think that is what's really special about it. It just feels like it encapsulated a lot of really special moments in my life.

”

Sabrina, on her 2022 album *Emails I Can't Send* and its personal significance, *Glamour*, March 17, 2023

I know that music has always been there in my blood and soul. I just loved the simple act of singing, the simple act of writing or the simple act of playing pretend.

”

Sabrina, on her love, and need, for music, upi.com, August 7, 2020

There was definitely a time in my life where I wanted to make everybody happy and I didn't know that the most important thing is to make myself happy.

Sabrina, on focusing on her own happiness, *Interview* magazine, May 25, 2021

I'm grateful for the people for tuning in, whether it be 10 years ago, five years ago, yesterday or tomorrow, in two years. There's definitely some people that are still not tuned in. I plan on tuning them in.

Sabrina, on her fans – old, new and in the future, *Paper* magazine, August 21, 2024

I only got to do two shows, but it was two of the best nights of my life. I cannot stress that enough.

Sabrina, on her two performances on Broadway as Cady Heron in *Mean Girls* before the COVID-19 lockdown, *Elle*, August 11, 2020

Someone listened to *Short n' Sweet* and said, 'It's almost like your music is a romantic comedy.' It felt like a weird way to describe it at first, but it makes a lot of sense. I think as a songwriter I do romanticize, but at the same time, those moments of innocence and humour are the moments that I find really special. Most of the time I think, nobody will find this funny, I'm just doing it for myself.

Sabrina, on combining her sense of humour with her music to make a sound that is genuinely unique, *Vogue*, August 3, 2024

I think there's parts of me in each song that represent me, but out of all of them, I actually like 'Mona Lisa' the best. It's one of those songs where I'm not thinking that much, and really just had fun with it. There wasn't a whole lot of production involved on it, and it's just so stripped back, almost unfinished and a work-in-progress, like me.

”

Sabrina, on her favourite Sabrina Carpenter song, "Mona Lisa", bakchormeeboy.com, April 12, 2019

I love being able to create something about what I'm feeling and know that someone in this world can watch it and feel inspired, feel a little less alone in their own circle.

Sabrina, on creating relatable art, *Forbes*, May 27, 2021

There's no point putting yourself in a box and restricting your own growth. We're constantly evolving, and I'm still very much finding myself... I'm excited for all the growth and lessons that still lie ahead of me, and maybe it's all just a matter of time before people finally see what makes me unique from everyone.

”

Sabrina, on discovering who she really is,
bakchormeeboy.com, April 12, 2019

Biggest pinch me moment? Mmmm, when Beyoncé knew who I was!

”

Sabrina, on the moment she thought she must be dreaming, katewaterhouse.com, September 9, 2018

I'm always singing. Like, literally, I never shut up.

Sabrina, on her love of singing, katewaterhouse.com, September 9, 2018

I would hope that if someone had never listened to my music before, and they listened to *Emails I Can't Send*, they would leave it feeling like they know me better as a person.

Sabrina, on the personal and intimate nature of the songs on her 2022 album *Emails I Can't Send*, *Vogue*, August 3, 2024

I deflect with humour, so it was only natural that a lot of the things that I was writing about – even some of the most painful moments of my life – were just so stupid, honestly, that it made me laugh. I was able to take these situations that really hurt me and use humour to cope with them.

”

Sabrina, on how she splices her now-iconic sense of humour into her songs, *Vogue*, August 3, 2024

I want people to be able to listen to my music and feel like they're wearing an outfit they love; it gives you that different posture, energy, attitude.

Sabrina, on how she wants her music to feel for her fans, *Marie Claire*, August 31, 2024

The first time I ever got sued, I wrote a song called 'Sue Me'. I've always been writing from that very real place. Taking personal situations in my life and being able to turn them into art was always a way of healing myself, and also understanding those situations a bit better.

Sabrina, on using her life as influence and inspiration for her art, *Vogue*, August 3, 2024

"

It's so cool for me to get a perspective on this whole process from Taylor [Swift] and the community of artists that I feel I'm close to – to get advice from them on stuff that you can't just ask the internet. We're always playing each other our music.

"

Sabrina, on having her contemporaries and peers, such as Taylor Swift, Ariana Grande, Chappell Roan, as friends, *Variety*, August 6, 2024

I ate, slept and breathed singing and would be at the piano all day. Even if I had nothing to do with singing in the coming weeks or months, I would sing just to practice and get better.

”

Sabrina, on her "practice makes perfect" mentality, whowhatwear.com, November 15, 2023

When I write a song and think 'I did not know that I could write that', that's when I get most excited.

”

Sabrina, on the unexpected joys of songwriting, interview with Lucy Rix, *Student Pocket Guide*, June 19, 2018

I think *Singular* sounds the most like Sabrina, which is one of the main reasons I called it *Singular*. I hope that fans hear these stories and they can relate. More importantly, the album for me has been very therapeutic in a positive way, because I think I was writing about situations which I was confused about or wasn't being positive about, and this turned them into positive memories. There are a lot of diverse themes and sounds on the album.

”

Sabrina, on the importance of her 2018 album *Singular: Act I*, *Student Pocket Guide*, June 19, 2018

Touring is never easy, I'm pretty honest about that, but my 2024 tour has been such a gift. This tour has been so much more fun than any other show I've ever put on. It's so theatrical and it involves the audience, so every night feels different, based off of how the audience is feeling and what they're giving to me. I was just blown away by the fact that it was my first arena tour, and we sold out every show. That was really overwhelming in such a positive way.

”

Sabrina, on the 2024 *Short n' Sweet* tour, *Vogue*, December 10, 2024

There's always gonna be stress, there's always going to be anxiety, there's always gonna be drama. But for me, being able to laugh at it all is really important. Also, caffeine.

Sabrina, on the two things she can't live without, *CBS News*, October 6, 2024

“

I’ve got to do what my head tells me to. I’m a bull inside.

”

Sabrina, on her determination and ambition, *GQ*, February 25, 2022

Sometimes it's a word I see on a billboard which is interesting and I go 'oh my gosh, this isn't just a word it's a whole story', and sometimes you also find inspiration along the way without really realizing it. I am so inspired by so many artists but especially the ones that are constantly changing, growing and pushing the boundaries.

Sabrina, on where, and how, she finds inspiration for her songwriting, *Student Pocket Guide*, June 19, 2018

I have no clue how I've gotten so many followers. Sometimes, I get a little sad when I share about organizations I'm passionate about and those posts don't get as much recognition or reactions as the selfie I took in the bathroom. It does frustrate me sometimes, but I try to curate my social media as much as possible to pick and choose what I do and don't share. But social media ultimately is just this distraction in our lives.

Sabrina, on social media, bakchormeeboy.com, April 12, 2019

"

The most mind-blowing thing for me is to see fans that I met when I was 15 years old. I see them now and they're going to college or med school or backpacking through Europe. Some of them I'm jealous of because it all sounds so fun. But there's so much beauty in the fact that we can all have a safe space with each other, and they've really given me everything. They've given me the ability to take risks and grow and make mistakes, and there's nothing more incredible than that.

"

Sabrina, on her fans growing up at the same time as her, *Hunger* magazine, March 22, 2022

CHAPTER FIVE

COMPLETE NONSENSE

She may be successful for her sultry soprano singing and her sparkly collection of corsets and go-go boots, but if you want to know the real Sabrina Carpenter, look no further than her now-iconic cheeky and mischievous sense of humour – a talent that sets her apart from her peers…

I feel like I have a very, very strong relationship with the universe and not even in an astrology-type or spiritual way. I think I've always just been very good at knowing the things that I want to do and that I can make them happen.

”

Sabrina, on destiny, *Cosmopolitan*, May 17, 2024

I'm definitely more like a cat. I'm smart, I love a little cat eye, I'm soft sometimes, I love a nap and I can jump. And I've got so many lives.

Sabrina, when asked "What animal are you most like?", *W* magazine, September 5, 2024

When I was younger, I definitely didn't think that my life would be picked apart in any sense, especially not my personal life. Like, I love Rihanna so much. I'm obsessed with Rihanna, but I don't care about those private parts of her life for whatever reason. So it's always just funny to me when people care about my private life – that's why I am just silly and sarcastic about it.

”

Sabrina, on her private life as public interest, *Glamour*, March 17, 2023

“

Emails I Can't Send was fucking sad, straight up.

”

Sabrina, on her 2022 album *Emails I Can't Send*, her first more adult project on a non-Disney-owned record label, *Time* magazine, October 2, 2024

The Famous Aunt

Sabrina isn't the only famous member of her increasingly legendary family.

Her aunt is Nancy Cartwright, the world-famous voice actor that breathes life into Bart Simpson, the unruly 10-year-old on the longest-running series in TV history, *The Simpsons*. For more than 30 years, Cartwright has voiced Bart and has become one of the world's highest paid voice actors.

"She's my dad's sister and a woman of many talents and always blows me away… We work at different ends of the industry, but I've learned so much just from observing her."

Sabrina, *Capital FM*, March 2021

I have so much respect for fashion. I feel like I've grown up around it, and it's such a big part of what I do. I'm a mess if I don't wear things I feel confident in. Performing is so vulnerable that if you don't feel 100 per cent good about what you're in, it's really hard to do it fearlessly.

Sabrina, on fashion and the importance of feeling confident on stage, *Glamour*, March 17, 2023

I don't think I should rule the world… I shouldn't be given that type of responsibility. I can rule my world, though!

Sabrina, when asked "You can rule the world for a day, what would you do?", *The Face*, February 25, 2022

Finding the beauty in everything is key, as is being able to not be upset when that beauty has gone.

Sabrina, on embracing both the positives and the negatives of life, *GQ*, February 25, 2022

"It can be so easy to be so hard on yourself."

Sabrina, on being her own biggest critic, *GQ*, February 25, 2022

Even in moments of free time, I'm always visualizing the future. Not to be the person that brings up their astrology, but I'm a Taurus, and I think that might have something to do with the fact that I've always just been very driven. Some people like to call it stubborn. I like to say driven. It's a blessing and a curse, as I would love to just be on a boat sunbathing somewhere too.

”

Sabrina, on her prolific workaholic mindset,
whowhatwear.com, November 15, 2023

The Bull

Sabrina's May birthday makes her a Taurus, a fact she mentions often in interviews.

This makes her prone to being stubborn, bull-headed and set in her ways, as well as a great listener and very dependable.

Tauruses are also extremely hard workers and never stop until the job is done.

Sounds about right!

I'm very lucky that I don't have people around me telling me what to do. I'm also a Taurus, so if they did, I'd get a little stubborn. I'm a tyrant.

Sabrina, on being her own boss, *The Guardian*, August 23, 2024

Femininity is something that I've always embraced. And if right now that means corsets and garter belts and fuzzy robes or whatever the fuck, then that's what that means.

Sabrina, on her stance on feminism, *Time* magazine, October 2, 2024

I feel like I entered Disney at a weird point where everyone else was growing out of Disney. I wasn't the lead of my show either, it was always very much an ensemble.

Sabrina, on her place in the Disney universe, *Capital FM*, December 21, 2018

I'm not a bird watcher, but I probably should become one. How awesome would that be? To just be able to spot a bird and be like, 'That's a crow!'

”

Sabrina, on the importance of having hobbies outside of music and fame, *Glamour*, March 17, 2023

I was talking to my friend earlier how my fans online think of me as like, a mother feeding her children! And I'm like, 'I'll keep feeding my children if that's the case. I won't let my kids starve!'

”

Sabrina, on always wanting to create fresh online content for her fans, *Billboard*, July 7, 2017

In 2018, Sabrina revealed the most important songs in her life that made her want to become a singer-songwriter.

1. "At Last" – Etta James
2. "Beautiful" – Christina Aguilera
3. "Rocky Raccoon" – The Beatles
4. "Dancing Queen" – ABBA
5. "The End of the World" – Skeeter Davis
6. "We've Only Just Begun" – The Carpenters
7. "Consideration" – Rihanna
8. "Smooth" – Santana ft. Rob Thomas

I feel a lot freer and more excited about what I'm making now because I've realized that genre isn't necessarily the most important thing. It's about honesty and authenticity and whatever you gravitate towards. There were a lot of genres in my last album, and I like to think I'll continue that throughout writing music.

”

Sabrina, on the creative freedom that comes from producing genre-free music, *Interview* magazine, February 8, 2024

"Everyone is going to have an opinion of you all the time, but at the end of the day, I try not to take it too seriously. Until you're face-to-face with me, it's not really real."

Sabrina, on online scrutiny, opinions and hate, *Seventeen*, July 11, 2018

I'm that kind of girl that will work until they physically pull me off set or out of the studio. I am very passionate and perfectionistic in many ways… but I always want the best of what I can offer.

Sabrina, on being a passionate workaholic,
Hero magazine, July 2, 2018

Being on stage singing is the same as acting – you're just telling stories. So much of acting is rhythm and timing – they help each other out in so many ways. I've had so many times where I've been on set and I've thought 'Oh, my knowledge from what I do on stage can help me' and vice versa.

”

Sabrina, on how her acting infuses her music, and vice versa, live-manchester.co.uk, June 4, 2017

For Christmas 2024, Sabrina released her very own Netflix special called *A Nonsense Christmas With Sabrina Carpenter*, or, as the singer herself called it – "A Christmas shit show" and "the ho-ho-ho-iest special of all!"

The hour-long show was recorded over two days and featured Sabrina's now-legendary wit in several comedy skits, much winking and twinkling innuendo and festive duets with friends, including Tyla, Cara Delevingne, Shania Twain, and a rather special performance of WHAM's "Last Christmas" with Chappell Roan.

I used to use the internet as a way to figure out the things I wanted to know, and now I find out things that I don't want to know... about myself, a lot of the time.

”

Sabrina, on Googling herself, *Seventeen*, July 11, 2018

I've always been someone that likes to change things up, and no project I've ever made has been the same as the one before it... or the one after.

Sabrina, on her passion for evolving her sound, style and songwriting, *Vogue*, August 3, 2024

My anxiety is probably my biggest struggle, and something I don't really talk about. I'm working through it.

Sabrina, on focusing on her own mental health issues, *Seventeen*, July 11, 2018

“

I’ve intentionally stopped myself from getting them now.

”

Sabrina, on no longer ordering espressos at coffee shops for fear of awkwardness, *Time* magazine, October 2, 2024

I'm stuck in the middle of somewhere between 'What is going on?' and 'I have everything under control.'

Sabrina, on her default mindset about everything going on in her life, Refinery29, August 5, 2019

I hate taking no for an answer – that's one of my biggest pet peeves – but sometimes that's what you have to deal with in this business, and you can't take anything personally.

Sabrina, on her persistence, *Cliché* magazine, December 9, 2015

I think that if an EGOT comes with the projects I put out with heart and passion, that'd be lit.

Sabrina, on receiving an EGOT* one day, Refinery29, August 5, 2019

* An Emmy, Grammy, Oscar and Tony.

I've been secretly married for eight years, nobody knows. I have a kid.

”

Sabrina, on her love of trolling her trolls, Refinery29, August 5, 2019

Sabrina's *Short n' Sweet* tour of 2024–2025 has become one of the most talked-about live shows of all time. Set in a two-story New York City penthouse, the show features 19 songs all set in various rooms of the house, including on the toilet.

For each date of the tour, Sabrina plays the party game "Spin the Bottle" to choose which cover song she performs. These are the songs she's performed so far:

"Mamma Mia" – ABBA

"That Don't Impress Me Much" – Shania Twain

"Material Girl" – Madonna

"9 to 5" – Dolly Parton

"Kiss Me" – Sixpence None the Richer

I'm always writing everywhere I go. If you see me saying something into my phone that's probably what I'm doing. I like voice memos. I like to write things into my Notes app. I think that's where I keep most of my writing ideas. I don't know what would ever happen if everything got erased. My whole life is in my Notes.

”

Sabrina, on constantly writing ideas for songs no matter where she is, *Buffalo News*, June 23, 2016

The worst thing about fame is that your little mistakes are magnified so much, and especially as a teenager, I messed up every five minutes.

Sabrina, on the negatives of being famous in the social media age, katewaterhouse.com, September 9, 2018

People like to make you feel like when you're above 21 in this industry, you're haggard. But I'm trying to remember that I'm still quite young.

”

Sabrina, on feeling her age, *Time* magazine, October 2, 2024

I'm literally 5 feet tall. So sometimes when I'm on that stage, it feels so huge that I just have to be larger than life in some capacity.

Sabrina, on her live arena and stadium performances, *Cosmopolitan*, May 17, 2024

Everyone's famous nowadays. There are dogs that have more followers than I do.

Sabrina, on fame and celebrity in the 21st century,
Marie Claire, August 31, 2024

Truthfully, if I wasn't in this industry, I don't think I would be on social media. Maybe that surprises some people, but it doesn't come as naturally to document my every move. I feel so much happier when I'm living in the moment.

Sabrina, on the dangers of social media, *Rolling Stone*, June 20, 2024

There's more to me than my hit songs. There's a person under there that some days feels really confident and some days literally just can't get out of bed. I think that's really important for people to understand, regardless of who they listen to, that they're a person.

Sabrina, on the real Sabrina, *Paper* magazine, August 21, 2024

I'm consistently evolving and growing. When you're this age, everything can change in a short period of time. I'm just keeping up with myself.

Sabrina, on riding the wave of her own evolution, *American Songwriter*, October 24, 2022